NOT EVEN BLACK

AND

OTHER POEMS

Howard A Fergus KBE PhD

© 2022 Howard A. Fergus

Published by Fergus Publications Ltd. 2022.

All rights reserved. No part of this publication may be reproduced or transmitted in any form without the author's permission.

ISBN: 9798835093168

ACKNOWLEDGEMENTS

Grateful to Delena Lynch Mason for designing the Book and the Cover and preparing the Manuscript.

Also by Howard Fergus

POETRY

Lara Rains and Colonial Rites
Volcano Verses
I Believe
Death in the Family
The Arrow Poems and Saturday Soup
Poems from Behind God Back
Obama and Other Poems
September Remember
March Montserrat and Hurricane Poems
A Word in Season, with St. Patrick's Day & Mango Poems
Our Mothers Dreamt
First of August Come Again: Poems of Celebration
Man Of the Match: Election Poems
There's Another Country: Poems From Sermons
A Matter of Life and Death: Poems
Lockdown Poems
Twilight and Glendon Poems

HISTORY AND SOCIETY

Montserrat: History of a Caribbean Colony
Gallery Montserrat: Prominent People in Our History
A History of Education in the British Leeward Islands
Montserrat: A Junior History
Festival at Fifty 1962 – 2012
Montserrat: Parliamentary Governance, 1951 – 2013
A Cloud of Witnesses: Some Pentecostal Pastors of Montserrat
St. Patrick's Day Celebration in Montserrat: A History

LITERARY CRITICISM

Love, Labour and Literary Criticism in Lasana Secou

AUTOBIOGRAPHY

Road from Long Ground: My Personal Path
Road from Long Ground: The Twilight Years

For

Coretta and Lucas
Oldest and Youngest of the Tribe

CONTENTS

Introduction   05

1. **Ourselves**

Gifting   10
Old Age Poet   11
Poet Of Gloom   13
Still Speaking   14
Humble - Really?   15
Learning To Lean   16
Covered   17
Noise   18
Family From Foreign   20
Labour Day Again   21
Old Fool   23
Slow Drivers Guild   24
To Run Or Not To Run   26
Manelva's Mission   28
Distinction   29
Birthday Wish   30
Longer And Stronger   31
Celebrating Life And Death   32
Let There Be Light   33
Favour   34
Mood   35
Evidence Of Aging   36
Teacher Howard Still   38
Legacy   39
Testimony   40

2.   **Others**

The Others   43
A Good Name   44
Eulogy   45
Happy Birthday   46
After Bishop Riley   47
Happy Birthday – Really?   48
Onward Still   49
Of Randy Greenaway   50
'Original Eye' Doctor   51
Befriended   53
Poet of Conscience   54
Naming   55
Belated But Not Late   59
Which Remedy   60
Three Shillings   62
National Pride   63
Women's Day   64
Romance   65

3.   **Not Even Black**

Not Even Black   67
From Far   68
Justice On Trial   71
Big Up, But   72
Nobel For Murder   73
Solidarity   74
Intelligence   75
Black Colonies Matter   76
Entitled   77
Not Even White   78
Platinum Holidays   79

4. Before Facebook

Before Face Book	81
Thank God	82
Why Holy Week	83
He is Not Here	84
There Is A Mountain Top	85
Who Rizpah	86
Double Dipping	88
Not Feeble Anymore	90
What Faith	91
Two Champions	92
As If We Didn't Know	94
Haunting	96
Labour And Bread	97
The Scarlet Thread	99
Evening Watch	101

5. Run Of Death

The Run of death	103
Dead Statistics	105
Teacher Vance	106
Captain Reid	107
Funeral Day	108
Wait A While	109
Invited	110
A So It Go	112
Healing Yourself	113
Thereafter	114
Post-Mortem Apology	115

6. Miscellaneous

Celebration	117
March 17 Celebration	118
Doors Shut In The Street	119
St. Patrick's Jump-Up	120
Tragic	122
Bad Word	123
Bad Wud Bishop	124
Put Down Lie	125
New Breaking News	126
Contradiction	128
Rotten Rich	129
Rotten and Rich	130
Too Soon	131
Hurricane Jingle	132
Under The Weather	133
Variety	134
Windfall	135
Air Power	136
Evil-Minded	137
Door Shut Excitement	138
Underbelly Of Beauty	139
Feline Break	140
Unhappy Mothers Day	141
New Crop	142
Worse Than The First	143
Wonder	144
Bush Doctors	145
Locking Down	146
Not Up To Mark	147
Passing Scenes	148
I Love Long Ground	149

INTRODUCTION

I will not boast in anything,
No gifts, no power, no wisdom,
But I will boast in Jesus Christ,
His death and resurrection. – Stuart Townend

This is the second major collection of poems that I am publishing this year consisting of over a hundred poems. Some poems make reference to my climbing years and my continuing capacity to write, and withal, my gratefulness for the gift and enablement. This accounts for titles like 'Gifting' 'Still Speaking' and 'Old Age Poet' in which "I balk at developing the reputation/as a poet of old age". These appear in the first section of the book, captioned *Ourselves* and is somewhat biological taking in other family members including my wife and latest grandson, Lucas whose life "…. promises to be a light/that is what Lucas portends/he has dreams to fulfill and an expected end".

The second section, *Others,* moves one away from self to recognize and highlight in verse, the contribution of selected others who have made a difference. In the arts Randy Greenaway and the irrepressible Dunstan (Conscience) Greenaway are included and one or two folks like Janey Winspeare of Long Ground, iconic at the people's level. In this section also, reference is made to Edgecombe, Edwards and Walkinshaw who with the famous W.H. Bramble formed the historic 1952 legislature under adult suffrage. The three are often omitted from the discussions. Even through poetry we can seek to put the records right providing it is not at the expense of art.

Section three includes the poem, 'Not Even Black' which gives the book its title. It treats with the Russian invasion of Ukraine where white people are on a barbarous attack against white, on this occasion; and it is a way of obliquely referring to the rampant racism which has been on display in the United States of America of late. The British threat to impose direct rule on their colony, the British

Virgin Islands at this time in history, naturally attracts satire. And on the positive side the occasional black achievement is sung. This section echoes the Black Lives Matter theme.

A person of faith with a strong spiritual heritage, this aspect of one's experience generates writings, and attention to it will not be denied. The section, *Before Facebook,* deals with assigning spiritual matters, the priority they deserve. Mild preachments come in here, whether they originate with the author or just the poetic version of someone's appealing discourse; the Rev. Dr. Bradshaw is a favourite. The poem, 'Who Is Rizpah', for instance, is about an ordinary Jewish girl who shines out from her sermon as a heroine, harbouring important lessons and deserving, one thinks, a celebratory poem. Sampson and Delilah attract a poem also, both champions in their own right, and is presented one believes, in an interesting light. And there is lasting memory of one's upbringing, remembering for example that:

> In Mission services in days gone by
> a frequent stock activity, was to rise and testify.

Dying seems to be one of the pastimes of Montserratians of late, giving rise to *The Run Of Death* unit which explores death without being necessarily morbid. It also draws attention to the death of notable people like Vance Amory of Nevis not omitting folk personalities like Montserrat's Captain Reid.

The final section, the usual *Miscellaneous,* contains some 31 poems of wide-ranging topics and interest. We made an effort to sub-group them in themes where possible. There are, for instance, poems of celebration linked somewhat with St. Patrick's Day, a big national day; three poems allude the dramatic smacking of Chris Rock by Will Smith on Oscar night accompanied by a big 'bad word …. that made the atmosphere at Oscar pregnant'; and unseasonal hurricane-like weather accounts for some pieces also. And in present day life,

Covid-19 has to affect the writing somewhere, and in the end, does so significantly.

As I may have said elsewhere these poems are the products of my mature years and are preceded by about 17 published collections. They are also emanating from a relatively long and busy life in the public sector and and civil society. My own life and upbringing in deep rural Long Ground is never forgotten, including the familiar title of respect, Teacher Howard. So in 'Teacher Howard Still' we have the lines:

> so teacher has stuck with me
> and in the mouth of the Long Ground constituency;
> for in their eyes it still carries dignity
> and they say it still with pride.

Some poems naturally deal with contemporary life, and one would hope that this area, along with one's life's experiences, makes for depth and richness of thought in the work. In fact the book ends with the nostalgic poem, 'I Love Long Ground' which briefly profiles one's patria and resonates with nostalgia;

Years of writing, reading and judging poetry should have resulted in a honing of the craft which is important for the enjoyment of the work. We no longer necessarily associate rhyming with poetry although skillful rhymes can add to the lyric quality of a poem. Some of the pieces do rhyme, in couplets, or abcb quatrains, and variations in three line stanzas. One hopes however that even where there are no conventional rhymes, that half rhymes, internal rhymes, rhythm and other literary devices, bespeak accomplished writing that is pleasing to ear, mind and spirit; and my mother is credited for bequeathing to me "the poetic mind".

For various reasons then, 'Not Even Black' may be regarded as a competent poetic work which, one suggests, could elevate, educate, and entertain. Not bad if an old age poet can achieve this. I am pleased to introduce you to the book, and do so with some confidence.

Howard A. Fergus
Lime Tree Lane, Olveston
Montserrat, May 2022.

1. *Ourselves*

GIFTING

Thank you Lord for this talent
which keeps on giving
like a co-operative cow which keeps on
yielding milk
at the gentle provocation of its nipples;
needing only short respites of rest
and nourishment in between
before the next harvesting.

Thank you for the interment stimulation
of my imagination
yielding rhythmic thoughts
that others had, but were never so expressed.
It is all a mystery
I do not fully understand;
but it is giving me the opportunity
to leave a legacy
in black and white as nourishing as milk.

And the act of writing is itself
an effective therapy
retarding mental deterioration
nourishing the creative 'let there be'.

.

OLD AGE POET

I balk at developing the reputation
as a poet of old age;
and that is not necessarily equivalent
to an old man writing poetry;
which is what, no excuse needed,
I have come to be, and do so thankfully;
but writing from experience,
it is difficult not to write your circumstance
and that of your contemporaries;
you write at least with some authority.

From this stand-point or situation,
you explore concepts like bed-ridden,
to discover it is a polite and euphemistic term
for when your bed becomes a prison
with the status maximum security
with limbs not willing to let you leave
without others' permission.

You are not on prison food
(and they say this is good in Montserrat),
but you maybe on a restricted diet
especially if you are afflicted with diabetes
that omnipresent malady akin to epidemic;
and bush tea from fever grass, aniseed,
and miscellaneous weeds
you may not have fancied at early morning
have now become gourmet drinks
with medicinal powers and reverence
for the elders, preservers of creole culture.

So sitting outside your door at evening
to watch the sun go down
is a precious pastime with the door
already shut in the street;
you count life's little, now big blessings:
that prints large enough exist that you can read,
that you are not yet locked down indeed.

You are grateful that your memory still ticks,
grateful you are able to reminisce
how God has been your Emanuel
throughout the years,
and has enabled you to do enough
to tap one or two joyful tears
especially over burdens you have lifted.

And bed-ridden may even harbour blessings
as unlikely as this may seem;
you are still able to commune and reason,
Heaven comes near and you can dream.

A poet of old age is no belittling title;
it is a privilege to write the ups and downs
(mostly downs) of the twilight years
of our elders; in the end, our common state of affairs,
if we are lucky or unlucky.

POET OF GLOOM

I've heard of prophets of doom
and do not want to be dubbed
a poet of gloom
but I heard another somebody
died right here yesterday, barely past fifty;
another somebody
from our dwindling population
and there's no particular joy
in being the minutest nation
in the ocean.
Even Covid-19 understand,
and has stayed its hand
when it comes to killing in Montserrat.
Yet still, (I don't know why we say, yet still),
another somebody went yesterday
and another one is threatening,
betting to go tomorrow.

And don't put goat mouth on me,
under your breath,
saying it could be he
and become a prophet of doom.

STILL SPEAKING

Last night, this late in life
I paraded centre stage to receive an award
like a bonus for being Speaker
for over twenty years,
like a last hurrah for the Honourable title,
however questionable the designation.
Like the spoken word, it comes not back
and if you dare to raise objection, as usual,
I will rule you out of order.
I was honourable for over twenty years
if it pleases you or not.

And please take your seat,
I am still speaking.

HUMBLE - REALLY
(For Sister Paulette, Montserrat/ London)

It is a source of great embarrassment
when people speak to you
of your great humility,
when you know in your heart of hearts
that your haughty mien and pretupness
stink to highest heaven.

But you are grateful that your penurious
past at Long Ground
brings you down to earth.

To confess your wonderful humility,
is to be proudest of them all;
one borders on the other
on boast of both you rise and fall.

If you have a happy story,
it may be God who deserves the glory.

LEARNING TO LEAN

So many times I leaned
on my understanding and fall down,
and still haven't learned
to put my weight on Him
in heavy life affairs.

So many times He is
my last resort
and I always come up short
when I should have leaned
on His wisdom in the first place
and not fall down flat on my face.

NOISE

Sometimes I am tired of the noise
indiscriminate cocks crowing in the neighbourhood
the same car on your lane,
with a sick muffler for months;
repeated photos on facebook,
certain poems included;
some of the tired repetitive talk
on the mind of the radio station;
CNN, Putin and Ukraine
and sounds of a new iron curtain;
the occasional ass, braying loud loud
and trotting out of tune.

Sometimes I'm tired of the noise
with my nuff and intolerant self;
ought to be glad I can hear,
to be glad that I am still here
and bray out loudly my blessings
instead of making noise, complaining.

And who knows, the cock fowl
and jackass may in their wisdom
think I talk too much, and should shut up.

COVERED

Now old and 'hard-back', I am learning
how some sacred writings apply to me
like that Numbers passage saying no magic curse
against Jacob or divination against Israel works.
In other words, you can't even obeah me.
God already has me covered.
So don't waste your money; maybe you can pass
just cut your eye and watch me black,
to ease the pressure lest you end up
with a heart attack,
for in Jesus I have comprehensive cover.

I am not gloating, but this is why
you came at me several times and failed.
He has the verdict fixed, not because of
any righteousness of mine but by the blood
of the divine one, through faith I am covered.

And don't bother to reap up all my sins,
he knows about them already
but has fully pardoned my iniquity,
the whole, not just in part.

I am beginning to understand
why all that hate and bitterness,
insidious weapons leveled at me
all my life, nearly all proved unavailing
and frustrating to the senders.
Not only were they not prosperous

as the scripture indicated,
but some boomeranged and hurt the sender.

So even now going down to the dust,
as the Anglican funeral lines say:
I raise the song hallelujah hallelujah,
God had me covered for eternity.

So don't hassle me. I'm covered.

FAMILY FROM FOREGN

I have a fresh excuse for living longer
in addition to the encouragement of my friends,
notably the readers of my verse;
a close family is visiting us from foreign
in October, touch wood, as they say,
because she was to visit us in March
when Covid-19 got in the way.

These days, there is so much humbug
on the journey: the mood of the weather
in collusion with global warming
and the health of the atmosphere
you are so thankful if you get there.

In the end longevity doesn't turn on your excuses,
rather on his benevolence and will
and perhaps the purposes you came to fill.
It is God who has to lengthen
the brittle cords of your existence
as Mission people pray and say
if we are to live another day.

Meanwhile I hope my pleading is not vain
to see my family who comes from foreign.

LABOUR DAY AGAIN

It is Labour Day holiday again
but my paper and imperious pen

will not take a respite
acting as if they were born to write,

conscious of the irony of labour day
a day for rest while getting pay.

There was this demonstration in Chicago
around eighteen eighty-six or so

resulting in a landmark revolution
and ultimately a tolerable solution

on the political matter of workers rights.
The capitalist kings had lost a fight.

By international consent
they fixed the daily working hours spent

to emphasize a freedom truly won
and Massa Day and slavery done;

but you could hustle and overwork
for extra pay and bulging perks.

So my paper and pen are in order
in spite of the holiday for labour,

to conspire with my imagination
to write a piece for the inspiration

of people who cannot live only by bread
but also on what the dreamers said,

receiving no pay in current currency
but a sense of satisfaction inwardly,

helping to celebrate Labour's day of glory
its relationship to management, a different story

with the age of serfdom fully over
though here and there oppression hovers.

So holiday work, these tools will not shirk
considering the time when none can work

not only because of loss of light
but our very existence is a fight,

and however strong, we eventually succumb
and must depart for our final home;

so we shall write until our day is done
on Labour Day holiday or whichever one.

To occupy ourselves and fulfill our calling,
we have to write whether night or morning

and plumb the mysteries of our time,
their hidden meanings and how they rhyme.

OLD FOOL
For Jamaal Jeffers

I breakfasted this early morning
on a poem by a friend, seriously witty
with the ancient wisdom of gran'-meres,
ending with this powerful line
of deliberate single-syllabled words:
there's no fool like an old fool,
a verity you've heard before;
but appearing now in this new dress,
it came as a fresh revelation.
I found it haunting, and immediately
dusted off my New Year's Resolutions
for a first amendment. With the epithet old
already in place, I vowed not to be a fool,
like drinking indiscriminate cocoa tea
for instance, and whatever comes with it;
for there's no fool like an old fool.
He is already damned.

SLOW DRIVERS GUILD

We have a surfeit of organisations
but I must perforce attempt another one,
inauspiciously named the slow drivers guild
where age is not a barrier.
Unavoidably slow driving
and ability to understand
are the requisite criteria
for a license to this geriatric band.

But you must learn to hold your side
and let the hurry-hearted pass.
There was a time when
you were more up to speed;
someone else can now take the lead.
Do not hog the middle of the road
that lane is forbidden at your grade,
we are not that important;
at this time of life, we are happy to be here
still fulfilling purpose without blocking traffic.

Oh and there's a fee,
these day nothing is free;
they take up a collection at burials,
at least that one is final.

Membership in the guild should buy you space
and following the rules can be a saving grace.

I appoint myself the President,
democracy is tedious at our age;
Vladimir Putin has already set the precedent
you can protest, but to your detriment.

TO RUN OR NOT TO RUN

It is too late to run in politics now
when I am even too feeble to walk
and though I still spin a good poetic line,
I doubt that I can talk the proper talk

of near Utopian promises
or dangle the sweetest carrots
before the face of the electorate
to captivate them and their votes.

It is not that the would-be ruling elite
set out to bamboozle people
their promises can be well meaning
but delivery may get higher than a steeple.

You attract the most vicious criticism:
no good, thinking only of themselves
Covid-19 and Ukrainian recession maybe abroad
but they shouldn't affect the national wealth.

And you getting a fat salary;
in your shoe, they would work for free,
they are just in politics for personal gain
couldn't care less about you and me.

The opposition can attract cynicism also:
all of them are same, it is said,
changing is only like musical chairs
the economy of the country will still be dead.

I respect the role of the politician
and those who brave the hustings to represent
and lead us; and encourage the politically
able to come forward with their talent.

But with a critical electorate,
we have to do the background work
and still come with broad backs to the forum,
vicious or benign criticism lurks.

MANELVA'S MISSION

I have accolades aplenty
and welcome them, justifiable or not;
they are, so to say, already in the pot,

but this call from Teacher Elva
by a few years my senior, was special;
her compliment seemed to tower above all

as she chose to recall at that moment
a little boy visitor to her neighbour in Cork Hill
unaware he had high destiny to fulfill.

At a teachers college in Barbados
she was already there and helped to mother me
that same little boy like an unspent penny.

She is now listening to me on national radio
releasing book after appealing book
well pleased, though the boy has an elderly look.

Her genuine applause tapped my tears
recalling, God like her was there all along
honing my life turning it into a song.

A timely reminder that lowly beginnings
pose no real barrier to success
when God has sworn by himself you are blessed;

that is the crux of that little boy's story
harbouring as he did more than met the eye;
treating with words he would be a blessing thereby.

DISTINCTION
(for Lady Eudora Fergus)

Laid up, I an sorry you were not present
in person last night, to receive your accolade
but a fruit of your own womb did it with style,
her dress apart. You were not there
but they spoke you fair although they forgot
you were a known net baller;
and a learned gentleman dubbed you great
with a straight face;
and other excellent epithets to decorate you
are being spilt outside the set citation
when I encounter many in the marketplace.
You were benevolent too, thoughtful and kind
are more expressive epithets of your helpfulness
to fellow travelers, your left hand
knowing only a fraction of what your right hand did.
So there are higher rewards to come,
below and above and you deserve them everyone.
You qualify to be called blessed by your children
whom you are leaving a legacy of a tall order,
an order of distinction. They'll have their own goals
but you will at least be an inspiration.

I was pleased that I was present;
and were this to be my last hurrah, I am satisfied
supremely to have witnessed this conferment:
The Order of Distinction by popular acclamation.

BIRTHDAY WISH

How do you say Happy Birthday to a loved one
ill and laid up for years
although there is the occasional event
that brings lightness, alleviating tears.

How do you say Happy Birthday to someone
who buried a younger brother the day before,
although memorials bring back memories
some precious, stoking joys galore.

And even in the darkest moments
one does recall the blessings of times past
albeit with a silent pity
that those seemed to have vanished oh so fast.

But on remembering God's faithfulness
and you a receiver of his enduring love
there is a yet wish for happier returns
when you will not be greatly moved

by what has been no light affliction
and what has gone on far too long,
a wish that you still hold on to your confidence
until one day, the victory song.

LONGER AND STRONGER
(08.04.2022)

Eudora is actually seventy-five today
outliving the number that the Bible says,

but since David, we are living longer
exploiting the loophole of being stronger,

and having access to better medical care
than was available yesteryear;

and though grateful for three score and ten
with a bonus five, we are not against

a longer run and a higher score
especially without the labour and the sorrow

promised to accompany long days;
like Moses, health wonderfully perfect, no decay.

That quality of life is wished for you now
as you go forward with hopefully a sunnier brow

sustained by the supernatural power of God
enjoying whatever good this life affords.

So Happy Birthday. Welcome to seventy-five:
family and friends are grateful you are yet alive.

CELEBRATING LIFE AND DEATH

From time to time
Life in sleepy Montserrat can be exciting
in its own way: like a brother and a sister
having a funeral, one day
and a significant birthday celebration
the following day
downplaying for a season
the flimsy curtain between life and death;
and the death of another family member
in distant Birmingham the very next day
sustained somewhat the emotion.

What would we do without the act of dying
to bring colour and variety to life,
providing stuff for poets. We dare not say
God doesn't know what he's doing.

LET THERE BE LIGHT
(21.03.22)

My grandson Lucas made his debut
to the altar yesterday for birthday number one,
receiving early blessings from the Father, Spirit, Son

with promise to return even if only
on the occasion of being born again
to secure not just the former but the latter rain

upon his life which promises to be a light,
that is what Lucas portends;
he has dreams to fulfill and an expected end;

so fellowship at the altar is the way to go
whether one built at home or in the sanctuary,
if he is to be a light and fulfill his destiny.

We add paternal blessings through the Three in One
as he ventures on life's winding upward way
hoping that he turns someone's night to day.

FAVOUR

Perhaps poetry and preachment
do not sit well together,
but a Sister Claudette Weekes provoked me
in my spirit this early morning
by asking God for favour
linking it with loving kindness
and including me among the beneficiaries.

Favour is a big deal,
you get what you didn't merit
what you are not entitled to;
getting it sometimes ahead
of others who are before you in the queue.

Loving kindness is big business too;
it is literally love in kindness,
based on nothing that you do
and is just part and parcel of the favour
a gracious God showers down on you.

So because His kindness and His favour
are better than my life,
my poetry shall praise Him
as I face the daily strife.

MOOD

When you are old, the external atmosphere
(a long-winded way of saying weather),
seems to have a greater effect on you;
the sky is overcast all day without rain
and grey, like a large umbrella;
the air is steaming though the sun
is not seen shining anywhere;
on the whole the sultry atmosphere
causes you to feel downcast
and somewhat out of sorts.

Or is it I who am imposing my downcast mood
and inner feelings on the elements
who are going through their routine
as is their natural wont?
I wonder who is reflecting whom
and whether the relationship is symbiotic
an image of the seamlessness of nature.

So if these dark, low hanging clouds
are harbingers of night, I must take the warning.

EVIDENCE OF AGING

If you need proof that you are on your way out,
decrepitness and lessened immobility apart
you need not look far: garments hanging
in the closet worn out from lack of wear
with rusty aging spots like choice freckles
confront you occasionally and your bulging paunch
if you are that way negatively gifted,
make some shirts and jackets look bad.
you are reluctant to bend over
to recover an object from the floor
getting back up can be big business,
a kind of Herculean labour ;
and drink soursop bush tea all you like
there are tired periods of insomnia
in the night a deprivation of vital nourishment
hurrying you along the corridors of recession.
Then there are old newspapers and primary source material
the stuff that make books are made of, falling apart
decaying like rotting flesh and I look at them
with sympathy and and nostalgia
and blame myself ungrateful for neglect.
And while so far defying dotage
to find myself at a funeral in two clearly
different colour sox was unsettling.
Hair colour is a normal indicator,
but you can't just count grey hairs,
for some black heads are really grey,
beneath, apart from the matter inside
and fears worries and vexation
can make your hair white prematurely.

You may be wonderfully long-memoried
when it comes to matters of the distant past
to discover that between hall to chamber
that gift has surprisingly faded fast.

Looking for proof that you are seriously
on the way, you don't have to look
much further; for whether you could read
and write or not, your eyes are dark
except perhaps when counting currency.

I will not rail against the all-wise maker,
but when they say old age is honour
I hope they know they talking for themselves
except like Moses they are gifted
with perfect or near perfect health.
Even so I am extremely thankful
to have reached this juncture in my journey
with the victories and disappointments
and enough sanity to reflect and write thereon,
 whatever happens down the geriatric road;
and may I make due preparation going home,
for the end which must come when it will come.

TEACHER HOWARD STILL

I accept the fancy titles
and they have served their purpose well,
but Teacher Howard is my Long Ground name;
teacher was a title of acclaim
back then, and gave me recognition as a somebody,
albeit born and bred behind God back;
so teacher has stuck with me
and in the mouth of the Long Ground constituency;
for in their eyes it still carries dignity
and they say it still with pride.
By that name I am still one of them
from their Long Ground, and we are forever tied
together and to our land of birth.

You may raise me up
and take me where you will,
but in sentiment and fact,
I am Teacher Howard still
of Long Ground with my navel string.
In the mouth of Long Ground people
Teacher Howard has a cozy ring.

LEGACY

Both a son and a grandson carry my Christian name,
so I must be careful not to defame

and dishonour them with a blot on their report,
causing them by my misdeeds to fall short

'just like their dardie' as detractors are quick to say
without evidence, just to wallow in my dismay.

This privilege carries with it the burden of living
not just for one's self but the blessing of giving

new generations a sense of pride in their forbears
and the challenge of passing on to their own heirs

an upstanding family reputation
which ultimately redounds to the credit of the nation.

You have already imparted elements in the blood
some to their advantage, others not so good.

On their behalf you are bound to good behaviour,
senior and forerunner, you owe them this favour.

So handing down your name is a serious legacy;
it is a pledge to avoid the very smell of rascality.

Name or no name there's an inherent obligation
to mind your put in the heritage pot for the little ones.

TESTIMONY

In mission services in days gone by
a frequent stock activity was to rise and testify

hopefully what you said was the whole truth
hoping it didn't damage your repute.

Prospect for a black Long Ground boy not bright
but God Almighty has a way of doing right

by those who put implicit trust in Him
regardless of pedigree or colour of their skin.

It is in this ancient spirit that I testify today
that God's favour has chased after me both ways:

When I lost a significant saving it was steep
but I somehow didn't lose a wink of sleep

while some in a similar situation went berserk.
I was sure that God the giver was still at work

on my behalf and I wouldn't beg my bread;
I was a seed of the righteous, as the word said;

not that I am never bothered by a sense of loss
but see it at the same time as another cross

and these are not uncommon on pilgrimage
often accompanying privilege

I have experienced his generosity in drought
as well abundant mercy when down and out;

so my testimony is a testimonial based on reason,
the God I choose to worship is God of all seasons.

2. Others

THE OTHERS

When Sobers and Viv Richards scored big innings,
it needed players down the order
to bring home the trophy.

On the seventieth anniversary of our parliament
the focus on star batsmen
the two Bs , Bob and Bramble is immensely in order;
but maybe we should spear
a ribbon of celebration for comrades
down the order, for their contribution to the team.

I speak of Edwards, Walkinshaw and Edgecombe
who came through in 1952,
making victory and a labour movement sure.
In addition to the big hitters, rightly dubbed excellency,
sweepers in the outfield are needed to bring up the score.

In my verse I include them in the lap of honour,
they also strove to give our people power.

A GOOD NAME
(For Rev. Toney Allen and Extended Family)

With eight children 41 grandchildren and 30 plus
great grands, this Montserratian matron,
of many names, all of them good,
Miss Christie, Caroline, Geraldine Gibbons,
went beyond her reasonable duty to the country.
With the the population at a dangerous minimum
her maternity has appreciated, as a larger population
is now a praemium for the viability of the nation.
Her demise brings a new sense of acclamation
for her fertile sojourn here,
fondly remembered for having wiped many a tear;
and of the little that she had with many mouths to feed,
they say she loved to share
thereby blessing other folks in need;
and she was diligent much the virtuous woman
according to criteria set by Solomon.
Many are still alive to call her blessed,
saying among our women, she was one of the best
and gave valuable offsprings to this land.

Hers is a Montserrat engaging story
now topped up by her recent call to glory,
where her good name has been written
numbering among the faithful and forgiven.

EULOGY
(For Kenneth Winspeare)

Mrs. Janey Winspeare of Tar River
(Wonder where that name came from?)
Long Ground's longest liver
finally left at 107.
Wife of the village butcher,
Rachael their only daughter
expert at blood pudding
has already gone before her.

I can still hear her voice at harvest time,
holding out long notes
as she "spreads the seeds and scatter"
at the Methodist cantata.

Dying in this seventieth year of parliament,
she is famous in her own right,
writing her live-long name
and the name of the Winspeare clan
in the Long Ground hall of fame.

HAPPY BIRTHDAY

Yesterday in church,
this man, his name is Abraham
boasted he was three score and ten
according to new birth protocol.

He was born again in 1952
the same year as the Montserrat parliament,
and like them he is still talking
albeit in the House of Lords,
I mean the House of God.

Happy seventieth Bishop Riley
wishing you many more return
so glad we didn't put you up
so we cannot take you down.

AFTER BISHOP RILEY

This business of a second birth
is a perplexing conversation
as Nicodemus murmured long ago
for him a logical and biological no-no;
and even Jesus the master teacher
did not deny it was a marvel
while admitting it had mystic meaning
like the motion of the wind;
we do not know its origin or direction
but see its unmistakeable effects.
So is the man who is born again
and is so transformed in spirit
'born from above' by inner action
everyone will see the change.

This is where I come out of the closet
to confess that I am glad to say
I'm one of them.
I too have been born again
knowing well the time and place
well over sixty years ago
Forgive me if my lifestyle didn't show evidence
of such a phenomenal experience
a second birth by the Spirit.

So I have cause to celebrate,
I no longer carry the weight
of sin and condemnation.
Like Bishop Riley, I have seen life
which teaches how to die.

HAPPY BIRTHDAY - REALLY

How wish Happy Birthday to a neighbour
queuing up for surgery in Antigua;
but the wish may well make sense
if they make her bleed to fulfill
a higher need for happier health,
giving her a new beginning
on the road to robust living.
.

So Happy Birthday Miss Dewar
there are no monsters in Antigua
you will be better for the journey
and your songs may well be sweeter.

ONWARD STILL
(For Dr. Joseph Jackman)

This classmate of mine of about equally ripe age
has accomplished much but is still very busy
with no plans to immediately quit the stage.

Imagine his delight to have heard from his doctor
after a thorough examination of his medical condition
that everything was well, at least with his pacemaker

which was pronounced good for fifteen more years
with such good news his heart skipped a beat;
from that sensitive quarter, there was nothing to fear.

This was no license to be careless the rest of the journey
with many dangers lurking on the winding road
ever throwing up new obstacles to kill longevity.

With so much left on his still to do list
in garden and house in art and craft
exploring his skill he has to eliminate unnecessary risks.

Nearing eighty-five, I hail his ambition
to make full use of his time whatever the circumstance,
with such positive outlook he is an inspiration

to fellow sojourners facing twilight
who may still have 'promises to keep
and many miles to go' before the final good night.

OF RANDY GREENAWAY

I doubt that Randy Greenaway has a mammoth
bank account, but he has given a favourable
account of his gifted sojourn in our land.
I therefore number him among our unsung
heroes, singing our island history
with melodious accent, and the colourful
romance of cotton fields white with slavery;
and the afterwards, with our fore-parents digging
their own graves in buckra fields to battle poverty
and elevate their children. He sings the road
to Long Ground, a pilgrimage of hard labour
carried out with fortitude and eyes fixed firmly
on the future; and there was a Long Ground road
in every village winding upward to a brighter future
for the children to come after.
For this laureate singer of the volcano, ashy Plymouth
was a seismic city and Montserrat was for a period
ruled by the seismicity of volcano, creating refugees
in we own country. He also wrote for artistes
who performed him at many a national event;
Randy was an artist-architect of development.
Home-grown archivist he lined up articles
and pictures - materials to write the island's story,
and with a liberal hand he shared the dusty treasures;
he was a trusty guardian of the culture.

I deem it a happy honour to sing a song for him today.
this unassuming giver, deserving of a rounder lay.

'ORIGINAL' EYE DOCTOR
(For Arietta Buffonge)

I was touched by this simple designation:
'original and best eye doctor'
(whatever the import of original)
to describe a native professional
on a sojourn of service
diaspora with a purpose
(however you pronounce diaspora).

It was a citizen's golden appreciation
of a citizen giving back to the island
for real, not just in rhetoric.

He had a purposeful run-up at cricket,
I do not recall his tally of wickets
as an island fast bowler,
but concur he is a damn-good eye doctor
proud of his origin
and we are proud of him.
(Please pardon the expressive epithet,
and the alliteration was alluring).

I almost omitted to mention his name,
Austin M. C. White
a black man accumulating fame
for servicing the sight
of his country looking forward to a 20:20 destiny.
We can boast of an 'original'
and yes, a best eye doctor;

this Montserratian rich in migrant history
with a mother born in Panama,
but he is firmly rooted home.

BEFRIENDED

In this extended season of dying,
I find myself harping on three male friends
of my higher learning years
who befriended me in life
and preceded me in death,
before I could repay my enormous debt
to them: Errol, Bradley, Edrick
of Erdiston, UWI and CXC
those academies of my success.

I console myself with a smithen of satisfaction
that all three in turn became welcome guests
at my Montserrat home before they left;
but still rue the thought that I bumped
into the death of two of them
quite by accident: a cause for lamentation.

Now in my recessional, looking to my passing out
ceremony and hopefully graduation,
their unmetred blessings resonate
causing me to wonder whom have I befriended,
albeit a little late
so close to journey's end.

And thoughts of the many others
the angels of my life of whatever gender
who in a multitude of ways ministered to me
on the road to where I am,
overwhelm me now, causing me to wonder

so close to journey's end
to whom have I ministered,
how many if any have I befriended.

The question is rhetorical
and anticipates no answer
inching towards journey's end,
it will be all up to the Master.

POET CONSCIENCE

Dunstan Conscience's today's satire
is hot like goat water on cassia wood fire;

and although I am now retired
I may not be outside the line of fire.

Hope he knows what he's talking 'bout
because a lawyer may find it hard to bail you out

if you present them with a very bad case
the solicitor's fee may be just a waste.

I myself am combing through every line
to see if any verbal assault is mine.

Whether he is speaking truth or calumny,
I deeply appreciate the poetry.

With the rhyming couplet he is masterful,
not even Alexander Pope will find it dull.

The scalding content is another matter;
it is serious transcending idle chatter.

But his gifting in poetry gets me,
to praise or satirize, the art is pretty.

NAMING

God reportedly mandated man to name
the living creatures of creation
and he named them right earning thereby
an A from God – the first; but I still wonder
how our fore-parents came up with such creative
and poetic names for places in and around
Long Ground. God calls them good,
I say appropriate, if He doesn't mind.

I understand Hot River heavy with Soufriere heat
and sulphur watering man and beast
giving its name to the whole environment
cattle pasture and cotton fields;
and Purchase speaks for itself resulting
from a lucrative transaction. Goolands
with its corruption of gold and goal
well fits a large and fertile stretch of land,
a rich prize, a play ground white with cotton.

You stopped at Mansilep (man slept?)
a plateau on the road to Roaches
where there might be animals to shift but in any case,
the landmark said you are almost there.

Cow River Bay was a special cove
on the east of the East where a river connected
with the sea in which we washed the clothes
of the dead as a rite on the ninth day
with limited bathing holiday among Atlantic stones.
It was here too that thirsty cattle

winding past higher ground at Turry Heart
came to water and give the bay their name.

At Bottom Long Ground you are even further
down than behind God back. You come from
Lulbow creole for Lo-debar a ghetto town
in scripture; the lowest of the low,
discrimination has long haunted some of us.

I don't know why Potter and Potter Ghaut,
(In Montserrat, a ghaut is a ravine),
which ran the whole length of the village
but we had our Potter people
who did not dabble in pottery or harboured
any paupers' grave. Potter may just have been
a cotton field owned by a Mr. Potter.
Our parents called it Potter and they were right.

Then there is Silk Cotton up the hill
a field of dreams before it became a unit
of the village, grudgingly, famous I suspect
for its lengthy silken cotton fibres;
and I never understood what they found
at Found Out, over on the other side.

But how did they come up with Lola Springs
like a line from a refreshing lyric,
with liquid gliding off the tongue
so alluring and desirable on a hot day.

It is humbling to think of our forebears
and their insightful naming skill
contemplating what we may have lost
from poets and creative thinkers, if you will.

If slavery had not dulled them.

BELATED BUT NOT LATE
(For Lavern Rogers Ryan)

On this your your advent day,
your borning day I mean,
friends overwhelm you with glad wishes
like a rejoicing stream,
happy that you are resident among us
making our own world brighter
by your infectious laughter and love of family.
To say you are a *people's person* is a cliché
but it fits you perfectly
like a garment made to measure;
but you are also a child of nature
one with bamboo and banana trees,
melting into backgrounds
that are innocent and green.

We thank the Almighty Maker
for putting you together
with choice ingredients in that frame
and hope that you continue laughing
to the very rhythm of your name,
serving ever in God's employ
and infecting your world with joy.

My happy birthday was long-winded ,
but genuine goodness was intended.

WHICH REMEDY

There are numerous prescriptions extant
for the island's remedy
from every kind of doctor, bush and academy:
from those who've run, the also ran
and those who cannot even run
except their mouth, like me;
and they have a right on paper
it is their entitlement
for in reality the ailing one is we.

Some want to bring old ointment
that has been tried and failed
convinced on the second or third time round
the old ideas might just prevail;
some are professional critics
whose voice must constantly be heard,
they are fluently on the record
though we nothing about their physic.
There is something rotten in the state
of Montserrat and they have the means and mode
they think, to set things right,
and will not rest; it is their patriotic duty
to bring solutions, minister to the island's plight
by their own hand and mouth, singly or in concert;
but their unpatented prescriptions
can be promising or paralyzing.

Now is the readying process, time
to reveal your ware, your medicine, I mean;
for those who now occupy the scene
will not surrender power readily

although the would-be new apothecaries
cannot attribute to them a single
positive treatment they have brought
to the marketplace: bruited as truth
as strange as fiction.

We welcome the new voices
whether crying in the wilderness or the citadel
they for the most part, wish our country well
not just their personal welfare;
but which of the pills to take,
in the mix it is not always easy to tell.
And the majority, they call them silent
know their know and keeping their own counsel
until the right time comes.
For as certain as there is balm in Gilead
there is medicine in Montserrat
and genuine physicians there.

THREE SHILLINGS

Back then at Long Ground when anybody troubled you
you threaten to put three shillings on them
at the Court House on Monday morning;
(A warrant cost three shillings at that time).

It struck me as a serious evil hanging
over someone's head to put three shillings on them,
and gave me a cautious fear of the court house
early in the morning and a desire to keep myself
out of politics, as the common people say,
meaning trouble of any kind that could be *lawyer wuk*.

Even today, a current of trepidation
runs through my breast and my heart beats faster
if I have to stand before the judge for any matter,
even not deserving of a fine or being put up in the locker.

I have not been uniformly successful at this,
but I have tried all my life and still trying
to keep myself out of people's politics.

NATIONAL PRIDE

I get an uneasy feeling when this little island
is referred to as a nation,
given its minuscule population.
I can understand island
as opposed to lane, drive or hamlet,
given it is a chance volcanic rock
with water all around it.

It is another matter to call it nation;
as though there should be a come-with figure
to deserve that designation.

Perhaps we should just settle
for our exoticism and uniqueness;
we are a nation with our headquarters
situated in another place.

WOMEN'S DAY

I love women from morning
ever since Eve
turned up to make me whole;
and I would not have it otherwise,
but I will abide what role reversal
may be necessary
to fulfill the nation's goal.

So I hail the equal sex and say:
Let the women have their day
to rue or vaunt their ascendancy.
Most times they are on top;
(in Montserrat I mean)
and working feverishly
to transform the feminine polity.

ROMANCE

Whether Vicky White shot herself
or were shot by her partner Casey
is irrelevant;
the story of their escapade
is the ultimate romance;
and an element of intrigue
would add to its appeal.

Related or not
they were both White
and their bond
in that Alabama prison was tight.

The story's end was almost perfect,
but for good or evil,
Casey White is left
maybe to give authenticity to the story,
plucking thereby from the mess
a sordid element of glory.

3. Not Even Black

NOT EVEN BLACK

The invasion of Ukraine by the Russians
is an event of apocalyptic proportion;

they are stumbling on dead people in piles
many shot down execution style;

it is World War One and Two rolled into one
with constant bombardment blotting out the sun,

killing women and children is fair game
this is war, everybody is the same

is the idiom of the century's butcher Putin;
in the pursuit of victory in war, there is no sin.

The world looks on watching Ukraine bleed
making your brother's keeper just a cheap creed.

Who could have imagined such a barbarous attack?
and the people of Ukraine are not even black.

'Trust this supposed poet to bring race into this';
I live in a real world; ignorance not always bliss.

FROM FAR

We are coming from far, Gold Coast and Nigeria
bought and sold like cheap bread fruit
ploughing for weeks through rough sea water,

jailed in the stinking bottom of ships;
daylight hid its face from us
dead freight fretting the wild Atlantic

before we reached the destination of infidels
white with oppression, turning out
to be overrun by cruelty, a veritable hell.

We were compelled to grow sugar
but life was not sweet, quite the opposite,
it was bitter like gall and green cassava;

we worked year round without wage,
we were owned by the master
we were treated like cattle we were low class slaves;

we were in bondage, church or school,
and the island was run by charlatan christians
who taught us to obey the master's rule,

saying slavery brought us to christianity;
they lied in the face of God
with the justification of iniquity;

for white was the colour of right
in black slave country. Perverting scripture,
preachers and planters generally tight.

When freedom came by whatever means
and it was not just Wilberforce; ask Eric Williams,
things not always what they seem;

we were not really free and we got not a penny;
the British compensated the planters handsomely
for losing us their very valuable property.

We coming from far from slavery to plantation
and metred freedom; like Michael Finnegan
slave children had to begin again.

In between child labour we managed some learning
not being congenitally inferior as propagated
but blackness dictated our state and earning.

And you are coming from Long Ground
long ways from town and water toilet
with grammar school out of bounds,

since your labourer parents did not hail
from a certain class and did not fulfill
certain discriminating details.

So we coming from far actually and in circumstance,
so even if you work your bottom off
you need raw mercy, and a glance

of favour from the eternal God who has lavishly
blessed me with gifts and opportunities
to counteract the inbred misery

of chattel slavery and its persisting aftermath,
giving me a sane self-confidence
negotiating life's still winding path.

With some success, I am mindful how far I've come
from ancestral bonds and bottom Long Ground
hoping to have sown seeds of freedom on the journey home

giving others the tools to think independently
so that coming out of servile tribulation
we can together sing the song of liberty.

We may sometimes fall short coming from this far
but downtrodden slave children are fully determined.
Like eastern wiseman, we have seen the star

and with our eyes trained on that promised haven,
where with all uphill wanderings over
we'll nevermore be heavy laden.

JUSTICE ON TRIAL

Black people were under fire in the person of
Judge Jackson for two days straight
in Washington which has no museum for slavery,
the Americans washing their hands like Pilate,
hearts still stained with the blood of blacks
condemning a people to the forgotten file of history.
For the Republicans, her confirmation or otherwise
for the American Supreme Court was a shameless
racist exercise with a veneer of politics
played out publicly on the platform of the world
for all to see what Lindsay Graham and the gang
were up to. I know Washington is politically partisan,
but a black woman keened the edge
of the attacks on this particular candidate,
and led to manufactured accusations approximating
ambush; they pulled out all stops to stop her
from fulfilling her rightful destiny.
But well armed with her sling of words like carefully
chosen stones and intelligent rebuttals, unfazed,
Jackson stood up to the giants on Capitol Hill
and brought the victory home to black people
of America and all over spoiling for advancement
in a world where black lives scarcely matters.

BIG UP, BUT

You have to 'big up' Madeleine Albright for her first,
first woman Secretary of State of the United States
topped up with US Representative at the United Nations,
signaling that the state of women mattered
at least twenty-five years ago when she shuttled
to and fro peddling diplomacy where big boys
used to play; and retired to teach it, the theory
based on practice. She piled up posts on top of posts
and numerous awards with Universities tripping
over one another with degrees in their hands.

But the cognoscenti are saying she had her weak side,
(underbelly would be an ambiguous word),
lacking as she did sufficient of the milk of woman
kindness to humanize her power.
Some Iraqi nationals are not applauding at her death,
branding the word 'genocide'. Serbians also
are questioning her humanity adding
minus marks to the great woman's legacy
suggesting perhaps she was not all bright.

I notice, me and Madeleine are match,
said in English, we have the same birth year,
but there the comparison obviously stops;
although my name is known abroad
throughout the Commonwealth of Montserrat.
She graduated from a different class.

Albright at least made an indelible mark for women;
that aspect of her life is not being seriously questioned.

NOBEL FOR MURDER

I wonder if we are leading up to a Nobel prize
for white cops killing unarmed blacks
in this God bless America, or its equivalent;
the prize going to the most abhorrent
execution and in the coldest blood.

It can be retroactive to include recent
artistic murderers who use creative instruments,
like the one who blithely kneeled on George Floyd's neck
while his life force ebbed away for the whole world
to admire or be outraged; and Eric Garner
who succumbed to a choice police chokehold
after protesting 11 times that he couldn't breathe.
The crude and cowardly April shooting
of Patrick Loyoya in the back of his head
is in the running also for a white police prize of blood

Perhaps these white campaigners for justice
via injustice, know something that we don't.
There's a constituency in America that glory
in the degradation of black people
and must be ministered to at whatever cost;
killing blacks grossly makes heroes of these cops.

A Nobel prize is going over the top,
but it seems to be a premium in America
for white police to treat black lives as trash.
Not all white police are wicked, I hear you
and agree; it is just that this is happening to blacks
too often and too often with impunity.

SOLIDARITY

Montserrat is time zone distant from Ukraine
but wavelengths of oppression encompass
oceans and guerrilla hills. The accent of our tongues
is nuanced differently, yet we who've sung
the mourner's song, sympathetically connect
to the distressed by the word made flesh.

I feel the keen of suffering in the ova of my mothers
and the stinging lash of whips on threadbare backs
under the merciless suns of slavery.

Suffering joins our hands over the bridge
of time and space and bathe them
in the gushing springs of freedom.
This word is my hand reaching out to you
and my hammer to smash the fastness
of the tyrant, shoot and kill his weapons in the long run.

I know to bear the big stick of the Barbarian
the fake justification of his action;
in a still unhappy way we are veterans.
We too have need of solidarity
in other things that matter
never mind the colour of our cause.

INTELLIGENCE
(For Jamal Jeffers and Prof. Murphy)

I acknowledge the 'mother' country
for its intelligence capacity;

when it locks ears with America,
they know when Putin poops in Russia

and therefore should have known
pro-royal sentiment had a Caribbean downturn

especially in Bob Marley's country
liberating itself from the colonial legacy

of three hundred years of slavery and racism;
royal visits no longer stir enthusiasm

except for anti-colonial demonstration
and renewed calls for reparation.

The young couple had to face the music
because someone at Whitehall doesn't 'get it'.

In the process they would have learned
a hard lesson of royalty spurned

and rejection of business as usual
with memories long on things colonial.

BLACK COLONIES MATTER

Whether or not the BVI Premier committed wrong,
I am surprised that Great Britain turned up
with the same old out-of-tune big-stick song

of direct colonial rule punishing an entire 'nation'
putting every one in a British prison
for one or two persons' indiscretion.

At one stroke they would disenfranchise
an entire population, putting power
in the hand of a Briton who is supposedly all wise.

Turks and Caicos and Grenada got a similar rap
some primitive years ago; but we've moved up
from first standard. This smell has to stop.

Such high-handed neo-colonial action
is highly out of place in twenty twenty-two,
and smacks of an insensitive administration

in the era of Black Lives Matter,
when systemic racism blanches the atmosphere
and fair play is what we have to agitate for.

The citizens of that country owe it their self-respect
to protest this indignity; they accept the rule of law
but this assault on the people's rights they must reject.

We salute the BVI in this lawful fight
against business as usual colonial might
We can think for ourselves and understand our rights.

ENTITLED

Montserrat staged no rites of passage,
but has come of age;
and is well known among nations,
assisted by natural disasters
like violent volcanos and horrifying hurricanes.

I doubt therefore, if it is entitled to claim
formal exemption from the pain
of the steep cost of living
fueled by war, the high price
of petrol, propane, and dasheen,
imported from Dominica and St. Vincent.

NOT EVEN WHITE

On paper we are British
our passport and nationality attest;
and that comes with some entitlement,
at least an annual largesse

along with help in national emergencies;
and they have scaffolded the budget
baling out their once rich colony
even if there always is a deficit;

and the Brits admit to their obligation
in the international arena;
but don't expect parallel treatment
with Leeds, Birmingham and even Gibraltar.

We can dream all we can of parity;
in theory we may be right;
but expectation could be a nightmare riding us,
and Montserrat is not even white.

We can exercise our lungs continually
demanding the same quality of pounds
that England spends on native children;
she is not 'blige and billy-bound'

to treat us with equality
or take ownership of our plight;
we are part of the dominion, Jubilee and all,
the part that is not even white.

PLATINUM HOLIDAYS

Our people love the Queen in Montserrat
as how I liked a calabash of moosha pap
at Long Ground.

Her obedient servants, since Britain
ruled the waves
at Plymouth and Carr's Bay,
are happy to close the island down for days
to big her up and her platinum ruling ways.

Not to be outdone,
I showed my pretty royal loyalty
by watching Trooping of the Colour
live on ITV;
over an English cup of tea.

And no one can outdo the Brits
on pomp and pageantry
or in Shakespeare's words,
thrice-gorgeous ceremony.

4. Before Facebook

BEFORE FACE BOOOK

At the dawn of a new day
it makes good sense to seek the face
of God before Face Book,
unaware of what you just might face
that very day
of good or evil;
seeing that He already knows the way
and the challenges you'll face.

A welcome is fully guaranteed
on the knees of grace,
as He himself has admonished us
to seek His face.

Indeed you just might need
the rawness of His grace
to face Face Book
a large file of miscellaneous information
and sometimes a minefield
that can blow your mind.

I confess my blindness
and vow to seek His face
before Facebook and after.
Forgive me labouring the point,
but Christ Himself sought His Father's face
before daybreak before Face Book.

THANK GOD

In a supposed Christian land
to openly give God thanks
for the supposed simple things of life
is no big belly boast,
or grand personal exhibition;
one is really showing-off the God
who stage-managed the success
in the first place. Honour is his by right
and giving it to Him I reckon as no robbery.

So let no one trouble me if in retrospect
I see Him there of old, orchestrating
my living like a symphony from early morning.
I blame myself for the discordant notes
that have come forth and thank Him
for the music of my life
that others with myself may have enjoyed.

So don't judge me harshly if I give God thanks
that my children all endeavour
to be law abiding, to take a single instance
of his innumerable favours.
It is His doing, all the way along;
and for all the blessings that have showered me
He rightly is my praise and song,
my lifelong good Good Samaritan.

WHY HOLY WEEK

I understand Palm Sunday and its message of humility
when Israel's king rode into the capital
on a donkey not a horse or mule
but establishing nevertheless, his right to rule.

Then Maundy Thursday and the respect for his religious culture,
as Christ celebrated the Passover again emphasizing humility
by washing his disciples' feet mandating them to love,
that central theme of Christianity that brought him from above.

Enters Friday the ultimate lesson of sacrifice
giving his love for those who loved him not
dying a disgraceful death upon a cross
a mammoth act of redemption for a world that was lost.

The essence of the Week seems to be love and self-denial,
scarce commodities in this present world,
although some do make a significant sacrifice for all of Lent
and give them selves over to pray and to repent

Perhaps the mandate of Maundy Thursday and the death
of Friday are the secret to a wholesome Christian life
teaching that to love like Christ and to be meek,
should characterize all our lives, not just for a week.

HE IS NOT HERE

He Is Not Here.
the statement dealt a sudden full stop
to the Marys who came to view the tomb
of Jesus on that Sunday morning,
is normally a disappointing one;
but there was nothing normal
about the death of Jesus and its aftermath.
He is not here: the answer gave
delayed gratification to the mourners
whose disappointment was afterward
transformed to victory. He was not there.

Four golden words depicting the position
of the resurrected Saviour has reverberated
down the years, replete with hope
for humankind. Through their import,
the struggle for eternal life is won or lost.
He is not here spells life after death
for the believer and God's love at an awful cost.

THERE IS A MOUNTAIN TOP

Martin Luther King saw the glory of the Lord
from the mountaintop
before his departure, before being stopped
by an assassin's racist bullet; and before him,
Moses saw the promised land of Canaan,
for us a shadow and a type of heaven
from the peak of Pisgah on Mount Nebo,
before his celebrity burial by God in Moab
in an undisclosed location.

Jesus too was transfigured before his death
in the presence of his disciples on Mount Tabor
and they beheld his glory which enveloped them,
as Peter later testified. And others
that we know in flesh and blood
have had the mountaintop experience
seeing their final home from afar off.

I believe there is a mountaintop for us,
a dimension of God's glory outside ourselves,
something transcendent linking man to God
and his eternal destination with a foretaste
and a foresight of wonder and excitement.

There is a mountain top for all God's children
and we can see his glory before we go from here.

WHO RIZPAH

There is this woman named Rizpah
no great name in holy scripture

with no pretense to be the virtuous kind
just another common concubine

belonging to the harem of the famous King Saul
who in Israel stood powerful and tall;

but he broke faith with the Gibeonites
thereby giving them legal right

to exact damaging reprisal;
so they killed Saul's family without burial

contrary to custom and culture in Israel
their dead bodies lay exposed on a hill.

Among them were two sons of Rizpah
whom she felt compelled to mourn for;

spreading her sackcloth on the rock,
she kept vigil for times warding off attacks

of birds by day and wild beasts by night
until King David heard of her sorry plight

and rescued their bones
so they could at last be properly entombed.

Rizpah in my book is a great mother of Israel
thanks to the chronicle, the second of Samuel,

devoted to her children in life and death
motivated by her motherly selflessness;

and thanks to preacher Bradshaw
for drawing my attention to tender hearted Rizpah,

this unsung heroine of holy scripture
who goes down in my book, an exemplary mother.

DOUBLE DIPPING

I am intrigued by how this St.Mark story ends
with a man being healed through the faith of his friends,

the incident happening in Jesus' own home
where people crowded to hear him, leaving no room

for this paralysed man who couldn't move a foot,
a prisoner to his bed his hopelessness absolute;

but he fortunately had friends who were people of faith
who trusted the Master whatever He saith.

Finding the house crowded they wouldn't be denied
so they devised a plan to get the man inside.

They climbed to the housetop and lifted off the roof
allowing Jesus to see profound proof

of their faith in His supernatural power
as they let the man down for his finest hour.

Getting more than he expected, Jesus forgave his sins
starting in other words at the real beginning

to the gainsaying of the religious purists
ignorant of the omnipotence of the Christ.

Jesus then ordered him take up his bed
which once carried him; he could carry it now instead.

Moreover, He ordered the paralytic man to walk
with some onlookers too surprised to even talk,

but the miracle could not be denied
it all took place before their bulging eyes

so they could not but give God the glory
as witnesses to the world of this astounding story.

Saved and healed, this man was double dipping
and Jesus called him son, he went home worshipping,

having earned himself a place in sacred writ,
a follower of Christ by grace with handsome benefit

through faith demonstrated by his fellowmen
revealing a truth outside the usual regimen

whereby we are admonished to have personal faith in God
if we are to receive the blessings promised in his word.

This man received the maximum through trust of others;
with an abiding lesson for those we call sisters and brothers.

NOT FEEBLE ANYMORE

I had a stomach full
with more than meat and drink,
as I sat around a large communion table
virtually, for the Lord's Supper this morning.
A Dr. Bradshaw was sharer and dispenser,
fully informed of what we were partaking,
and its long term effects; it was not fattening
but enlightening; it is a rite, alright
but brings with it consumer rights
like those enjoyed by the Israelites
after the Passover meal in Egypt
and were miraculously healed of all defects
before they started on that epic trek
destined for the land of Canaan;
there was not a single feeble one among them.

In the Lord's Supper we too have rights
as we were rightfully instructed
for the Passover was a foreshadowing
of the cross and the Lord's Table;
so as we we eat and drink we are empowered
to do whatever before we were not able.

Having partaken by faith I am not feeble
anymore. I have had my fill
and met once more the Christ of Calvary's Hill
amply strengthened for the journey.

WHAT FAITH
(For this very reason, make every effort to add to your faith….2 Peter 1:5)

I like the idea of faith as a way of being
according to preacher Warner; in reality the cornerstone ,
the real root, grounding any good deeds shown;

it is fundamental to Christian living
not just an episodic now and then belief
for a now for now relief

in a time of crisis or a negative encounter,
although that kind of faith certainly matters;
this is the faith you live by and constantly follow after.

The recurring chorus: Have faith in God
is a sane and sensible admonition,
but living out your faith is a critical decision.

This kind of faith can develop, as you add
moral excellence, godliness, self-control
and brotherly love, not selfish like this world's.

It is no embarrassment to be a person of faith
endeavoring to fulfill all righteousness,
at once a beneficiary of belief and be a soul at rest.

TWO CHAMPIONS

Israel's Samson and Delilah of Sorek Valley
in Philistia were in a strange way evenly matched
(I don't mean the kind match
that is sometimes made in heaven; theirs clearly wasn't).
They were both champions in wiliness and wisdom ;
he artist, adept at composing riddles and she,
a champion at devising tangling schemes.
Both were fiercely loyal to their country
with Samson adding physical strength
giving him the upper hand supposedly,
if you discount the deadly power of love,
and a woman skilled to wield that weapon.
With Samson's godly purpose to deliver Israel
from Philistine bondage and Delilah's bent
to silent his superhuman strength pitted
against her country, a battle of two giants
was truly on the cards. In the end,
love and the woman's lap
made all the difference; love tied Samson up
in knots and cut his Rasta hair,
causing his miracle strength to disappear.

Through prayer his hair began to grow again
like showers of a latter rain;
and although he killed thousands of Philippians,
it was through a suicidal act which left Israel
still in bondage, according to John Milton.
So though Sampson fought a punishing battle,
albeit blind, it was Delilah who ultimately won;
and 'Israel still served with all his sons'.

I make no inference about a woman's power
or a man's susceptibility to a scented flower,
observing only that in spite of the gifts of Sampson,
it was Delilah who finally came out champion.

AS IF WE DIDN'T KNOW
(For Rev. Dr. Ruthlyn Bradshaw)

This preacher held forth eloquently
on Sunday as is her wont; her text:
"There is a God in heaven" echoing Daniel
a Hebrew exiled in Babylon faced with a labour
more difficult than Hercules'. His lord the king
demanded to know the meaning of his troubling
dream as well as the dream itself, on pain of death.
No man was ever known to accomplish such a feat,
but Daniel answered readily : There is a God
in heaven, as if we didn't know. He however
knew what he was up to; in two twos time
he called an old-fashioned prayer meeting
with his three home town friends, and God
answered promptly out of heaven and revealed
to him the vision of the king and the interpretation.
This led to a stay of execution for the cabinet
of Babylon and the political elevation of Daniel
and his compatriots, God raising up whom he wills,
proving that He rules in the armies of heaven
and among the inhabitants of earth and no one
questions his authority as the scripture states.
This was a confirmation of one's personal faith
that there is indeed a God in heaven,
the inexhaustible source of power and resource;
and if that were not enough, it was played out
in my own experience the following day
when God showed up unexpectedly in a person
that I desperately needed to see and another

that needed me. There was a God in heaven
whose will is also done on earth, for him and me.
So I say Amen to Daniel's universal declaration
on the existence and omnipotence of God
and his involvement in the affairs of earth.
The reminder of that Sunday preacher was timely.
There is a God in heaven, hence the miracle
that I am, coming from relative obscurity
at bottom Long Ground to mountaintops of glory.
There is a God in heaven who elevates.

HAUNTING LYRIC

The words of that morning meditation song;
'come as a wisdom to children,
come as new sight to the blind',
tear and tare me up
and is still haunting me at evening.
So I confess my simplicity
and reliance on the Holy Spirit
no matter how many or what degree
I may accumulate.
I need his wisdom to negotiate the dodgy straights
of life even the seeming simple on the surface.
Dependency on my educated understanding
has landed me in trouble oftentimes,
and I am not even wise enough to learn from my missteps.
The revelation that I am not as independent
as I pretend to be, has prompted me
to join the chorus, raise the plaintive prayer:
'come as a wisdom to children',
as in humbleness I learn to know my place,
as I confess my ignorance and blindness.

LABOUR AND BREAD

As the sun sets on another Day for Labour
I recall Holy writ says much on the subject,
even associating it with God's disfavour

when man was driven out of paradise
condemned to eat bread by the sweat of his face
hard labour alone appeased Lord and Christ;

so hard work itself became a virtue
making laziness a shame and misdemeanor
committed by persons without a future.

All work for a living can be dignified
whether academic or manual labour
and with due recompense recognized.

Calling on the thief to mend his ways
Paul gave him an honourable motive
to go and occupy himself in work that pays

so he can do good to someone in need
instead of preying on the honest worker
to fatten his selfish greed.

Jesus himself had a busy work schedule
was a good time manager working while it's day,
diligent, he obeyed established work rules.

We are enjoined to work for another bread
one that doesn't perish and even here,
labour is necessary, to be spiritually fed.

So Labour Day is in sync with the divine will;
God himself worked, giving meaning to rest,
and labour for whichever bread, is necessary still.

So Happy Labour Day in whatever cotton field,
we are still to work while it is day;
a benevolent Master gives the yield.

THE SCARLET THREAD

I am familiar with the harlot Rehab
and the story of the scarlet thread;
but the way this preacher put it over
would bring the lifeless from the dead.

Among the lowest of the low in society
this woman had divine insight of two Israeli scouts
sent to spy out the land of Canaan
before launching a total rout

of what would be their future homeland.
For their safety Rehab gave them accommodation
putting their mission before the interest
of her country; but agreed on serious compensation

When Israel's army invaded Canaan
Rehab wanted the lives of all her family speared;
and to distinguish their dwelling they advised her
to hang from her window a scarlet thread,

reminiscent of the Israelites in Egypt
who had to place blood on the lintel of their door;
this was a vital secret sign of safety
to allow the death angel to pass them o'er.

Rehab implicitly obeyed the spies
and at the crucial time exhibited the scarlet thread
and on the morrow of the invasion
not one member of her family was dead.

This symbolizes the cover of the blood
and the amazing miracle of the cross
if our scarlet sins are not under it
we are destined to suffer loss.

By the miracle of that scarlet thread
Rehab was transformed from harlot to saint
proving that no one is too wicked
for the blood to save as long they repent;

and save them from the worst to the uttermost;
and as evidence of its efficacy
the name of the prostitute Rehab
shines out in red in Jesus's genealogy.

EVENING WATCH

It seems like a cliché like 'going forward'
but sitting on my patio at an over-ripe age
(it is not so long ago, I was just force-ripe),
I thank God that at evening I can watch the clouds
craft themselves into various shapes like fluid sculpture
as if they know what what they are doing;
and the leaves romancing gently with the wind
against a backdrop of green trees of various shades,
corrugated hills and a pale blue sky,
together an entrancing scenery with night
creeping in, threatening to blot out it all,
as if on a grudge assignment;
and my pen itself understands something of evening,
that period before the lamp goes out.

And I wondered where it all goes to,
till I remember well that after night
somewhere must come the morning
which gives me hope
for a new day with a rosy dawning.

5. Run of Death

THE RUN OF DEATH

Death has always dogged us from the beginning
whether by acts of murder or by natural passing.

The poet David deftly described life's transitoriness;
for him it was a hand-width or just a breath

or even a shadow vanishing readily with the sun;
though we busily accumulate wealth for some, anyone;

Like our parents we are travelers passing through
and because of sin the death penalty is soon due.

It is the rate at which we pass that rattles us now
called out by the umpire before the How?

Some before they settle properly at the crease
before their come-with competence is released

as if we are rushing to catch a final train
and before our sun is in its zenith, we are drained

of life, prematurely harvested as they say
from God's garden because of love, hardly the way

we understand that word: not a harbinger of grief
for loved ones left behind, more like a thief.

So we stand aghast at the rapid pace at which we pass
hoping to God this bumper crop will not long last

and accept that death isn't going anywhere soon
but hope our people's night doesn't come at noon;

it makes sense to prepare early, not last minute
to meet our final enemy with the sting taken from it.

Whether we die untimely or live the perfect score,
John Milton says the ways of God are just for sure.

DEAD STATISTICS

We continue to pile up corpses
as if it were a new industry
and the diaspora is co-operating to swell
the dead statistics of their country.

We create euphemisms to air the sad event,
they are not just dead and gone or passed;
we wax lyrical in our announcements
they are a family limb broken off.

Born and die are too pedestrian
sunrise and sunset are figurative and sublime,
the funeral is a celebration
part of which is a repast time.

But the statistics keep on piling up
as if we are tired and long for rest
and it is not just old ones who are leaving
your schoolmates, along with age subordinates.

We pray for slowing of the funeral train,
a lull in the undertaking traffic;
they have to make a living but island population
growth is now an important building brick.

TEACHER VANCE

Vance Amory didn't take Out easily
when he was at the crease.
To our regret he is now without question
gone for good; not for good, I mean.
(You see how the English language humbug-up)
I mean his innings is now over.

He is a beloved son of the Nevis people
having played well for them
at school in politics and cricket;
he was a good all rounder
and could have used a longer stint
but was called out today.

The people of Nevis are standing up
all over the pavilion to honour him;
they believe that he was not only called out
but called up to higher service,
and Montserratians who knew him
are keeping faith as well,
active as he was in church and state,
regretting, that all so soon his wicket fell.

CAPTAIN REID

I used to wonder who was Captain Reid
and did not at all realize
it was someone I had known for years;
what's on his mind was transparent;
he spread goodwill to family and friends.
I wondered who was this captain
and of what ship
or maybe it was just a large friendship.

Now the radio which he frequented
has published his sad passing
leaving many in the cold
robbed of his sunny greeting.

Simple simple so, Captain Reid
endeared himself to Montserrat
and worthy now to be remembered
for his cheering voice and cheerful chat
wherever ZJB is heard.

No MBE or OM trails his name
but he is a celebrity just the same;
to die on his wife's birthday, a little much
but consonant with the icon's ironic touch.

FUNERAL DAY

Today is funeral day for David Edgecombe
as his ashes for real, collide with dust
in his mother's grave
in his fatherland;
funeral day for her older sister
a main mourner
and a number of others of his tribe.

People of plays are mourning too
because he had put Montserrat on the stage
to international applause
and he treated with the media also,
putting other people on stage.

We regret his funeral day
a little premature
according to the general rule,
but at the same time we're assured
of his worthy contribution to the artistic culture
of the nation.

Today is funeral day
and with the rush of late
towards the departure gate,
someone else is going under with him,
albeit separately.
Today is funeral day for David Edgecombe
and we are sad to see him go.

WAIT A WHILE

Crowned with grey hairs,
sitting outside Glendon hospital
across from Casualty,
an undertaker passed
and gave me a broad bright smile,
innocently, I know.
But with my perverted poetic mind,
I wondered, merely wondered
if he saw me as a prospective customer
someone to soon put under.

Although he will have the final smile,
by God, he has to wait a while.
Not going everywhere in a hurry,
but then you don't really know
and the reaper has been very busy lately.

INVITED
In Memory of Judith

It is a most doleful story
as strange sometimes as truth
invited to another land
to attend the wedding of a friend
and be killed en route.

You didn't even get to take your *dan-dan* dress
out of the grip
or catch the bride's bouquet
betokening that you are next in line
to adorn a wedding day,
or fit into the picture to prove
you were a witness
to the covenant, and wined
the wedding feast away.

Now all this is but fantasy,
the ironic stuff of poetry.
But so glad you have also been invited
to the marriage supper of the Lamb
who has provided you with a *dan-dan* dress,
clothing you in His righteousness.

This does not cancel the sadness
of those you suddenly left
who will long bemoan the manner
and untimeliness in which they are bereft.

But you are in that other land
so many of us have in view
and by one means or the the other
we are en route there too.

A SO IT GO

The death of this young lady
this awkward tragedy,
an accident on a Guyana road
with delayed action for maximum agony,
still weighs heavily on me.
She had done loads of good already
garnering a following and fans;
but that is no excuse
with so much in the world to do
and labourers few; there was still much use.

There is so much we still don't understand
about whether there is chance or accident above
(and up there, I do not think they shove),
or everything is predetermined
by some hidden love.
It is all a mystery to me.

But for now until we know,
we lick our wounds
and with a shrug of shoulder,
tell ourselves: A so it go.

HEALING YOURSELF
(For Rev. Bethan Murrain)

You lost your husband
the only one
just two years ago
and now a phone call tells you
that your daughter also has passed on,
the only one.
What words will console you,
alleviate your pain
when your pillow is a stone
and your pallet has in bones.
Pray, what words will reach you,
heal the hurt
except what you yourself have preached
from on top the pulpit
to others in distress.

Physician heal yourself
is not always a kind injunction;
but we believe that the God
whom you proclaimed and walked with
all your life, who also is the Comforter
will not now let you down;
that his sufficient grace abounds.

THEREAFTER

The word abroad is that the morgue
at Glendon hospital our only accommodation
for the dead prior to their departure
is overcrowded, due to heavy traffic
in the dying business of late.

Covid-19 has to take some of the blame
as loved ones coming home for the funeral
are required to quarantine for days,
thereby postponing burial
with a longer stay at the facility
as a consequence.

We are fortunately not fussy
at that stage,
but can still use some dignity
at this antechamber to our final resting place,
en route to eternity.

They say that when we are dead we're done
but we must still build for the living
and thereafter, if you get my meaning.

So if you are planning anything
(Don't tell me to speak for myself),
you may wish to think about our now facility
and the thereafter.

POST-MORTEM APOLOGY

I apologize ahead of time
to those who are omitted from the list
of persons left-to-mourn at my sundown
as they cozily say these days,
either inadvertently or because of glut.
Pardon the conceitedness but you are just
too many to call, before we get to
the "too many" clause in the announcement protocol.
(That's what you get for bathing me in humbleness),
and I am not in any competition
for the longest line of mourners
on the loaded mind of ZJB.

I prefer to make much of you now
for the generosity lavished on me
above ground, heedless of my unworthiness.
This epistle comes to warn
you are no less esteemed for being omitted
from the list. You are already wonderful
and left to mourn,
whatever the paper didnt say.

I am spelling out your name
and our undying relationship
in my imagination, in this poem,
written near St. Patrick's Day.

6. Miscellaneous

CELEBRATION

I was there from the beginning and I ought to know
that some forty years ago
we began to sing the heroes of St. Patrick's day
who showed Montserratians how to bleed
for freedom one red day in seventeen sixty-eight.

So what an excellent way for me to celebrate them,
to release a book about their celebration
hoping that Miriam's timbrel and the drumming never stop
from north to South in a grateful Montserrat,
proud of golden moments of their history
in spite of the stubborn trappings of a sordid slavery.

What a way to remember those teachers
and the children who remembered
them, instructing us to know our past,
like Edith Allen Mary Griffin and Joy Nanton
who first taught us to celebrate Christmas in March.

They caught the imagination of a thankful people
who looked beyond the bacchanal
and transformed a significant event
of their history into a continuing festival.

MARCH 17 CELEBRATION

I was thinking of some way
to celebrate this Saint Patrick season;
and I don't like wearing green
for no compelling reason.

My jump-up days are over
which frankly never started;
so I will cut my hair, to make me look trim
and trim my lawn
as a mark of respect to the warriors of 1768,
heroes of Montserratian martyrdom;

Meanwhile I celebrate the recognition
that martyrdom is still in fashion
in this mini innocent island.

DOORS SHUT IN THE STREET

The Bible sometimes speaks
in allegories and figures;
and you may have to read between
and underneath the lines
to divine the meaning;
like when Solomon says of aging
that the doors are shut in the street.
I now know from experience
he is speaking of access and communication;
as I decide not to drive down Fogarty at night,
as a prelude to not drive at all,
when my jeep is permanently parked;
then whatever is wrong or right
with my thinking and theology
or my creaking limbs, for that matter,
my doors are shut in the street,
my doors to the street are closed.

ST. PATRICK'S JUMP-UP
(17.03.22)

I don't jump up
and it would not have crossed
St. Patrick's mind.
Not that I think it's wrong
if you do it right.
But in my circumstance
even if I were to wine and go dung
there's no coming up for me
slowly, and may be not at all;
but I miss the early morning sounds
of celebration in the air,
and jovial vibrations in the atmosphere,
feet pounding pavement
and bodies bouncing against each other
in delicious dance.
Even a visiting St Patrick
would have enjoyed a glance,
and like me may be missing the jump-up,
this St. Patrick's day, not averse
to a break of levity
on this special mutual Holiday.

Music or no music
Montserrat's murdered martyrs
are still jumping up for joy in spirit
that the light and music of their sacrifice
will ever live for generations to inherit.

So I jump with them today
to the music they engendered
on that sad Holy Day.

TRAGIC

There was high drama
at the Oscars last night,
but it was no play
and no one was acting
in spite of the melodrama
when Will Smith smacked Chris Rock
with powerful expression
using exotic tongues
that echoed across the world,
for an allusion to the illness of his wife .

Chris Rock's may be king of comedy
but the episode smacks more of tragedy,
with an undetermined hero, on a night
pregnant with significance
for decorum law and order.

BAD WORD

Will Smith made the atmosphere at the Oscars
pregnant last night
with that big bad word
that the television normally out-outs
for decency. In polite circles
we say expletives
and indecent language.

I don't know if a precedent has been set
for Presidents Premiers and others of the elite
to crack bad words like slavery whips
to spice up speech,
driving home the meaning
and put the cover on a box.

And will there be a culture shift
laundering foul language
making it innocent for use in schools
as in Hollywood.

That classic slap still resonates
with untold repercussions
and the performers have gone down in history.

In the end, who the hell I think I am,
to say bad words are bad.
I yield to the wisdom of the Academy Awards.

BAD WUD BISHOP

Ever since Will Smith stirred things up at the Oscars,
I can't get bad words out of my mouth,
my mind, I mean, Bad wud was a colourful
and common expression in daily life.
Fluent speakers of the tongue
were ordained bad word bishops,
because bad word was their Bible
and their mouth was nasty;
their language brought them notoriety
even if it did not qualify them for an MBE.

Those for whom it was an occasional speak
would instantly ask you to pardon their Greek,
and the conservatives deemed it clever
to merely threaten to ask you the island favour.

Poets sometimes getting into creole,
finding them artistic let one or two fly
as did the great Derek Walcott when 'de wailing
kiss-me-arse flutes' brought water to his eye.

So bad words came in forms and fashions
you spit out the ones which connect with your passion
trying not to go overboard
as Will Smith did at the Academy Awards;
even if the four-letter choice went down well with a slap
in polite society, you have to know where to stop.

To control bad word will be ever a problem,
as they taste so sweet to those who use them.

PUT DOWN LIE

They say Putin telling lie
about Russian troops around Ukraine
but big people don't tell lie
especially somebody up so high.
So they must be telling untruth about the man.
But if NATO and American intelligence think
that his lying is a true belief,
he needs to put down lie and take up tief;
and that could be another calamity
if he assaults and robs Ukraine's sovereignty
landing us in World War III.

Putin will use any excuse
to keep Ukraine from joining NATO
his alleged lying is a ruse
to justify invasion and bring his bigger purpose through.

To be honest, high class lying is not confined to Putin,
Some American politicians also major in that sin.
At least is so they say.
And their British relatives across the pond,
we cannot leave them out,
they say these days 'nough lies
fall from their mouth.

NEW BREAKING NEWS

In three days of breaking news
Putin is breaking Ukraine apart
with guns and guided missiles
creating ghettoes of refugees
in Slovakia and Poland
while their patriotic men and women
fight with all their heart
training guns on Russian soldiers
spilling opposition blood and filling
body bags for export, giving
not as good as they getting
or as bad, but going down fighting
with their wounds in front,
in defiance of the bloody tyrant
with an outrageous appetite
for expansive power at any cost.
This bull is in the ring with a little heifer
while all the world looks on
with all their might,
their arms between their legs,
almost, avoiding world war three.
What a way we spending millions
killing one another with some people dying
for want of a cup of soup.

With Russian tanks parading in their capital
Covid-nineteen looks like an ally now
compared to Putin's military muscle
essaying to pulverize a people

and build a red kingdom with their ashes.
He is a disease of the likes of Hitler,
a megalomaniac hooked on power
with his own people cowed in subjection
arresting and locking away free speech.
He is calculated to win the war,
but will he win the peace.
That should be answered with a
resounding No by people of goodwill
everywhere where freedom reigns
and sometimes e'en gets out of hand;
for uncharted freedom can be burdensome
like democracy running amok.

Meanwhile we stand in solidarity
with the good people of Ukraine
or fall with them,
though we can't exactly feel the pain
inflicted by an unfeeling despot
who has padlocked his people's tongue,
those aghast at his inhumanity,
with tons upon tons of artillery
on the heads of an innocent people
with breaking news breaking them
continuously, albeit with stout resistance.

CONTRADICTION

To say that I am in denial is a contradiction;
but for Montserrat to jump
from zero case of Covid-19
to perhaps the top per capita number
in the world, is incredible.
So I don't believe it.

Those of you who like me
are in denial, need to work
to bring the numbers down
and prove our skepticism right.

Meanwhile, I am in denial
on the 98 new cases,
and calling for a revision of the numbers
and a reduction thereof.

This is more than a play with words;
we may be into a national crisis
if remain undeterred.

ROTTEN RICH

I hate clichés
but Her Majesty the Queen is rotten rich.
If her son Prince Andrew comes up short
in pocket or, behaviour,
she can bail him out
ten million times and over;
she is the rotten rich owner
of the Duchy of Lancaster;
and because of his connections,
the Prince is also rotten rich.

ROTTEN AND RICH

Vladimir Putin is both rich and rotten
reckoning his wealth in sprawling homes, aeroplanes
and disgraceful dollars in big banks abroad.
Most nations of the world are now regaling him
with ignoble epithets like rogue and pariah,
and isolating him, as if the great man
were inflicted with a peculiar strain of leprosy.
Like a mad man without human feeling,
he has unleashed Russian military might
against Ukraine's civilian population
on provocation he himself trumped up,
(the pun on trump was unintended),
slaughtering even children in the process,
although Putin found that nation no push over.
This has put him quite beside himself
and he has now threatened to go nuclear
like the barefaced criminal he already is.
He needs to be captured urgently and caged
lest we become engulfed in global war.

Vladimir Putin is not only rich and rotten
there are signs he may now be off his rockers
to the world's collective detriment.

TOO SOON

There was a restless gusting of the wind last night
accompanied by slanting sheets of rain,
you would have thought it was already June;
and when I was growing up
that month was itself deemed too soon
for these high-handed hurricanes.
So why is March blowing up such a fuss
with so much already out of order
down to flour they say is scarce ,
we are lucky it isn't toilet paper
as it was once upon a time.

So the month of March should take a break
and not blow itself out of breath,
already causing a loss of my dozen
out of season Peter Kidney mangoes,
not the windfall I was hoping for;
with the Putin world war still a threat
and Covid-19 still creepy in effect.

But maybe I'm making a poem out of nothing,
it is just nature doing its work
and we ourselves are sometimes out of order
blowing our top even unprovoked.

But I still say in the hurricane moon
that March and June are far too soon
to threaten us with such big winds
except to give me a poem out of nothing.

HURRICANE JINGLE
(Traditional - Adapted)

June, yes, too soon
and not the right moon.
July, pass us by.
August, there is no must
for wind and water.
September, remember
not to linger in our quarters.
October, pass over
in a light breeze
November, defer to December;
just freeze.
December is not a member
of the hurricane brigade;
we are no longer afraid.
Time to jump-up and thank God
our country has been speared.

UNDER THE WEATHER

The sun was under the weather
this past week at once a means and mirror
of our own depression and displeasure
as it allowed dark clouds to roll in over us
greying our lives already heavy
with the high price of war in Ukraine.

The sun is shining in its glory today
beaming with cheerfulness
putting us in a better mood to face
our gloomy circumstances.

This reminds me of a brighter Sun
which once sojourned in our skies
with its lowing clouds, and knew our sorrows;
he is destined ever to arise
with healing in his wings and a brighter weather.

VARIETY

I don't remember these March and April winds
but hesitate to put them down to global warming;

because somebody has acquired a bad name
you cannot heap on them every blame.

A notorious thief in the community
does not mean is he who scamps your coconut tree

at nights, or distress down your potato ground;
you may be well way out of bounds

to swear it is that neaga man John-John
when it could be some other respectable man.

Maybe the wind is just nature vaunting its moods
at will; showing it too has an attitude,

not unlike some of us who sometimes blow our top
surprising those who didn't know 'a so we stap'.

We can enjoy the winds in their various measure
airing the variety of nature's treasure.

So global warming or not, winds are welcome
to cool our temper to blow away flotsam;

or maybe to sanitize the atmosphere
with sickening bugs turning up everywhere.

WINDFALL

Selected branches of my burdened
Peter Kidney mango tree
(not sure where the name came from),
waved a refreshing promise of a March windfall;
but before the wind could make them fall,
ravenous birds seized them,
five at a time, and heedless of my famine,
their feasting never stopped.
They cleaned the seeds white as hungry children
did with their teeth at Long Ground
polishing them to the stone
while I helplessly looked on.
Birds of the air you can't take them to pound
for their home is everywhere
and you grudgingly admit
God sends bread for man and beast;
and their feasting never stopped
so instead of a mango windfall
you settle for mere bird drops.

AIR POWER

These birds flaunting their air power
like Russia,
are attacking my zaboca tree
devastating every fruit and flower
without discrimination.
Europe will not assist
against this superior force;
so I will ask the English
and maybe Montserrat
to help me drive away these Russian birds,
these inhumane barbarians
from my avocado tree.

EVIL-MINDED

My pair of zaboca trees are busy
for the season burgeoning with blossoms
accommodating scores of bees, butterflies
and wasps pollinating for the harvest
getting ample payment in kind, living off the land.
But bad-minded birds short sighted
from my point of view
impatient for the harvest, are raping
the tender flowers in their cradle
denying the bounty due to me as owner.

It is just not fair (but who said life was fair)?
The birds because of their air power
attack my property from above
wasting my blossoms and infant avocados
to feed their hungry maw;
and might not always right, as in Ukraine.

I have to be content with their left-overs
which last time were pitifully few,
and perhaps a lousy poem.
Not right (but life not always right);
we negotiate it existentially,
and the bees and birds too, I suppose.

DOOR SHUT EXCITEMENT

It doesn't take much to excite
when the doors are shut in the streets.
This past week was exciting:
I made national prime time news
suing in court for a lenient sentence
for a young fellow citizen
(and ZJB is not an idle organ, I suppose).

Days later two white policeman
arrested my siesta using flattering words
not to arrest me thankfully,
to prize evidence out of me for a criminal matter
putting me in politics, as Montserratians aver.

And the dead are not left out;
on Saturday three funerals were on stream,
one in England, two in Montserrat
at the same time and I attended all.

Doors shut in the streets is not imprisonment;
they open occasionally,
and you are pleased that in your active life
you used doors profitably.

UNDERBELLY OF BEAUTY

You wouldn't think they were pests,
these beautiful
black and yellow worms
with pink stubs for feet
snaking from leaf to leaf
feeding in my garden
and breeding butterflies,
reminding of the face of evil
which is often beautiful
until it bites.

Prettiness can be in cahoots
with ugly tricks
like the underbelly of beauty.

FELINE BREAK

Two cats, one brown-inclined, the other black
strategically stationed, or so it seemed
at the entrance to this Hilltop cook shop
closed for Sunday. You wonder
whether to keep away man rats
or just waiting patiently for the opening
and a delicious meal of scraps.
Were they feeding off their fat
while they kept vigil knowing by now
that they too must observe a day of rest.

Perhaps I underrated them keeping guard
a job well done waiting for their just reward
however long it takes,
understanding well the necessity
of a cook shop break and stomach on recess.

UNHAPPY MOTHERS DAY
(For Sonja Smith et al.)

Mothers' Day is indeed a happy
annual celebration that both mothers
and the children revel in,
and happy treasuries give thanks.

Some even send greetings to their mothers
up in heaven,
as those who've gone just happen to be there;
and mine had better be,

after all that praying, tithe paying
and walking on long dark roads
to the house of God, when drive to church
was not yet invented.

But there's an unhappy Mothers Day
constituency
whose mothers are late,
having left them far too early,
and who are never catered to
in the happy ceremony
and the spree on Mothers Day.

I have seen some with lines of sorrow
on their faces, and send them
kind regards on Mothers Day,
belatedly.

NEW CROP

We thought we had put paid
to Covid-19's growth in Montserrat
but we now have more than a ratoon;
it is new a crop trained on our children
in a strategic move by the pandemic
to ensure maximum growth and large scale
affliction of the body politic.

We must now orchestrate a proper response
beyond trading blames and putting
another white mark against the government.
Perhaps there is a case
for judicious personal management,
for Covid-19 is not child's play.

WORSE THAN THE FIRST

At over 330 positive cases and currently and climbing,
Covid-19 was rampant in the capital today,
(I mean from Cudjoe Head to St. John's).
Some Covid shops were totally on lockdown,
some scantily staffed, and the testing lines
at St. John's clinic critically feverish and long;
and with very few hungry for the vaccine
the reign of the virus promises to be strong.
You can always bank on customers
to be in the single national bank,
but today the lines were lonely,
the tellers few and relatively silent.

School children were in something of a wonderland;
their baby sitters, teachers I mean,
were not late but absent, permission irrelevant
in this covid dispensation; with the education sector
hard hit, both children and adult population
seriously afflicted by slow learning.

Covid-19 is rampant in the island today,
maybe tomorrow and the the next day,
and we have to live with it, the authorities say;
as with the price of dasheen from Dominica.

This rise of the virus is worse than the first;
it is anyone's guess who will feel it most.

WONDER

It is a sad Saturday night
in this Covid-19 country
when a sapling succumbed
to the virulent virus.

Her spirit sped away
leaving us to ponder
and to wonder
oh so many things.

Her early passing;
should at least be a warning.

BUSH DOCTORS

Growing up in Long Ground
I am familiar with bush tea
but I am wary of so many bush doctors
flaunting their idiosyncratic remedy
for Covid-19.

I am not opposed to a potion
of ram goat bush, fever grass and aniseed;
but live or die, I am abiding by the medicine
of the trained physician with the Hippocratic creed.

This is not necessarily a rejection
of creole cure and bush science;
just my pret-up preference.

LOCKING DOWN

Covid-19 is locking down the island
shop by shop and early stop
with no official announcement,
just effectively ad hoc.

There's no violation
of the government's 'live with' policy
just a sensible coping strategy
like dressing to suit the season,

But government policy or not
Covid-19 closing down Montserrat.
I hope I'm wrong,
just another prophet of doom;
(we have a surplus of these already)
Time for Covid to give us room.

NOT UP TO MARK

I am not feeling wonderful today;
'not up to mark',
my mother would have said;
but I will do whatever necessary
to hold on for now.
And to be honest I am in no break-neck
hurry to depart;
With the mango season
just about to start,
there is a luscious reason
to delay some;
the end needs no prompting when to come.

I may not be feeling up to mark,
but there may be many hours left
before the dark.

With so many responding to the announcement
with prayer, to wish me well,
it warrants a postponement
of the tolling of the bell
to a time that only He can really tell.

Until then I occupy
and write my heart out.
I continue to make my mark
while light is still about.

PASSING SCENES

It is the last of March
and end of the first quarter
of a year no longer new,
to be followed by the first of April
in a matter of hours;
months pass like scenes
in a living drama
of different genres and divisions
carrying our lives away;
one day, a play of passion
whether of love or anger
causing comity or separation,
another of comedy and laughter
the atmosphere made lighter;
there are epic moments
of troubles overcome
and hard fought victories won
with the occasional tragedy in between
testing our human weakness
with survivors even in disaster.

It is a life of passing scenes
and ultimately
we ourselves, pass from the scene.

I LOVE LONG GROUND

I love Long Ground and would not be born
in any other space. The baritone music
of the wild Atlantic drowned whatever was forlorn.

Long Ground is not behind anybody's back;
we read the face of God early in the rising sun
and feeding ourselves we had no major lack.

Short on currency, we made good on kind
and had no need for baby formula. With arrowroot,
corn, moosha and tous les mois pap we were just fine.

We grew yams and pumpkins of many shapes and sizes,
and green sulphur dasheen like those that now commute
from Dominica, but at more delicious prices.

Strong, we carried loads of wood and water
on our heads which surprisingly left room for learning
long division sums, and preparation for hereafter.

In order to receive a modicum of learning,
we travelled on foot for miles to Bethel;
and this particular house of God was not always loving

if you were not Methodist. Liberal with the rod
teachers didn't give you 39 stripes like Christ
but you suffered to reach any decent standard.

By my time, teaching had become more civilized
and many of us made the mark in spite of,
and Bethel earned a good name in our eyes.

Long Ground now appears on many a stage
in governance, arts and oratory; it will be difficult
to erase our name from history's page.

Two churches ministered to the spiritual man
and folks with a higher taste for worship
sweated up hill to Harris' to the Church of England.

A village of masquerades, cantata and church concerts
we were colourful in the performing arts
in which all mingled, the good-inclined and seasoned converts,

loudly supporting blood family and wanting more
with "our side our side" slamming pennies
on the table, to purchase encore encore.

Our elders performed and recited sweetly
although many had barely reached standard two.
My mother bequeathed the poetic mind to me.

Her sleeping place is now out of bounds
but I would have liked to be buried near her.
I belong to that same soil, I love Long Ground.

I get sentimental and almost teary-eyed
as that humble village resonates with me;
I was born in Long Ground on a happy tide.

Made in the USA
Columbia, SC
14 October 2022